# Choc Chips for Mum

By Sally Cowan

T0360192

It is Mum's big day.

Tam's mum likes choc chips.

So Tam gets a big pot.

# Tam gets nuts and figs.

4

Dad has a choc chip
on his chin!

"Did you scoff them up?"
said Tam.

Tam tips the choc chips and all the bits in the big pot.

Then she can mix it up till it gets hot.

Pip and Bun hop up.

Sniff, sniff!

Tam puts a lid on the pot.

Tam got a hot bun.

Dad got a big mug.

Then Tam got the
choc chip mix.

"Yum, yum!" said Mum.
"I like choc chips a lot!"

# CHECKING FOR MEANING

1.  What did Dad do with the choc chips? *(Literal)*

2.  How does Tam know Dad has been eating the choc chips? *(Literal)*

3.  What do you think *Mum's big day* might be? Why? *(Inferential)*

# EXTENDING VOCABULARY

| | |
|---|---|
| **choc** | What does *choc* mean? Is it a full word or a short form of a longer word? What is the longer word? |
| **chop** | What does Tam use to *chop* the nuts and figs? If you take away the *ch–* digraph and use the *sh–* digraph, what word do you make? |
| **where** | What sound does the digraph *wh–* make in this word? What other words do you know that begin with *wh–*? |

# MOVING BEYOND THE TEXT

1. Why do lots of people like choc chips? Have you ever used choc chips in a recipe?

2. What would you do for Mum or Dad on their special day? Why?

3. Have you ever eaten some of the ingredients or mixture when someone else is cooking? What did you eat and why?

4. Why should you have an adult help you when you are cooking?

## SPEED SOUNDS

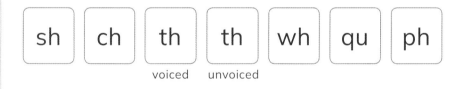

| sh | ch | th | th | wh | qu | ph |

voiced  unvoiced

# PRACTICE WORDS

chips

choc

chop

chin

them

Then

chill